They had been taught
by their mothers,
that if they did not doubt,
God would deliver them.

ALMA 56:47

WHAT LATTER-DAY

Stripling
Warriors

LEARN FROM THEIR

Mothers

Ardeth Greene Kapp

Deseret Book Company
Salt Lake City, Utah

ISBN 1-57345-164-9

Printed in the United States of America

10   9   8   7   6   5   4   3   2

To my beloved and noble mother,
Julia Leavitt Greene,
and to the mothers of the sons and daughters,
latter-day stripling warriors,
who served in the
Canada Vancouver Mission
1992–1995

Acknowledgments

I express appreciation to our beloved missionaries from the Canada Vancouver Mission, 1992–1995, who willingly shared their tender feelings concerning what their mothers had taught them. I'm thankful for my husband, Heber, whose inspired leadership contributed to the spiritual growth of those young men and women.

My sisters, Sharon Larsen and Shirley Burnham, and their children provide rich opportunities for me to more fully appreciate and understand the sacred role of motherhood. I'm grateful to them.

My appreciation goes to Sheri Dew, vice president of Deseret Book Company, for encouraging me to share what I learned from today's stripling warriors. Thanks also to Emily Watts, editor, and Kent Ware, designer, for their help in preparing this book for publication.

*S*pring was in the air, and new growth was everywhere evident on a beautiful Sunday morning. The parking lot in front of the church was a whirl of activity. Young ones were receiving last-minute instructions from their mothers concerning proper conduct for stake conference. At the same time, those mothers were straightening little boys' ties and arranging little girls' curls before releasing the children to the eyes of the stake members. Older children bolted ahead, leaving younger ones trailing behind and parents bringing up the rear.

In one area of the parking lot, a young man, almost deacon age, was resisting his mother's efforts to straighten his hair. She put her comb to her lips to add a bit of moisture in hopes of taming his unruly cowlick. Only after he looked just right did she reach into the car and place in his arms a small bundle, the newest member of the family. With his hair straightened and his arms extended, he received the trust of his mother and the responsibility for the baby, if only for a brief time. He walked proudly, eager for his treasure to be noticed and his maturity recognized.

Could these be the boys whose mothers combed their hair in the parking lot just a few short years ago?

Near the chapel, an elderly man struggled to get his legs out of the backseat of the car. With patient assistance from his daughter, he finally stood upright, steadied himself, and then looked around with a smile of gratitude. Gently waving his feeble arm, he greeted all who were passing by on their way into the chapel.

As my husband and I were entering the front doors, two young missionaries with scriptures in hand stopped to visit with us. Looking at them, I wondered, could these be the boys whose mothers combed their hair in the parking lot just a few short years ago? One of the elders pointed out the stake president's sixteen-year-old son hurrying past. "He will make a great missionary," the elder commented. "He has a lot of his dad in him."

Being acquainted with the diligence and dedication of those two missionaries, I was thinking that each of them must also have a lot of his dad in him. Then the idea came loud and clear: Yes, they did have a lot of their Father in them.

So does each young man and each young woman. All of us can be great because we have a lot of our Heavenly Father in us. "We are the children of God, and as His children there is no attribute we ascribe to Him that we do not possess, though they may be dormant or in embryo" (George Q. Cannon, *Gospel Truth,* 2 vols., compiled by Jerreld L. Newquist [Salt Lake City: Deseret Book, 1974], 1:1).

All of us can be great because we have a lot of our Heavenly Father in us.

I became very interested in observing the stake president's son that day. Yes, his appearance was very much like his dad's. I watched him make his way through the crowded chapel to the front, where he took a seat on the second row, next to his mother. The early morning sun was streaming through a side door, casting a warm glow over the bench where they were sitting. The prelude music ended, and the stake president stood to welcome everyone. While I listened to his powerful spiritual message, I watched his son and the boy's mother as they sat together. Questions tumbled from my mind like apples from a barrel. Had the stake president once sat in conference by his mother? What part had she played in his preparation for this very day? How would that legacy be carried on by his son? The most memorable sermon for me that day came not over the pulpit but rather from the sidelines, from watching a young man and his mother. There was no question, just as the young elder had stated, that the president's son would make a fine missionary because he had a lot of his father in him. But, according to divine design, he also had a lot of his mother in him. Her influence during the early planting seasons of his life would surely be felt in the harvest to come.

One evening more than twenty years ago, standing at the bedside of my three-year-old niece, Shelly, I pondered: When does the preparation for motherhood really begin? When do mighty souls become great mothers? What of the space between here and there? At that time, I penned these few lines concerning that memorable experience and my unanswered questions: "All her other dolls had been lined up with care and placed aside. But at the close of the day when all was quiet, clutched in the bend of a fat little elbow was Sweetypie. Sweetypie had all the hair worn off the back of her head; one eye was missing, and one arm was almost detached. Yet there she was, tucked protectively under the arm of three-year-old Shelly. Standing in the twilight with the last rays of sun filtering through the shades, I looked long and thoughtfully at the quiet little girl now at rest from play. Almost reverently I rearranged the covers as I bent down to feel both her warmth and that of Sweetypie. At that moment I thought I was witnessing the beginning of a miracle, and I marveled at the beauty I saw. When is the season for gathering, acquiring, and developing? What of those attributes, skills, characteristics, and spiritual promptings that all become a part of the greatness? When do all the

When does the preparation for motherhood really begin?

qualities of motherhood, the myriad bits and pieces and combinations of beauty come together? When does the divine kaleidoscope take final form, so that no matter which way it turns or which parts are exposed, the pattern will enrich those who encounter its beauty? Whence springs the spiritual reservoir from which all members of the family may one day partake? Surely Sweetypie had some place in the marvelous beginning of this preparation. As I left Shelly tightly holding her treasure, I continued to ponder about the space between here and there."

Over the past twenty years as I have sought for a deeper understanding of this miracle God has placed within reach of every righteous woman—according to his time and purpose—an accumulation of insights, impressions, and awakenings has come to my mind. The past, the present, and the future, so close together, seem on occasion to be beyond reach of time. Shelly one day released Sweetypie

When does the divine kaleidoscope take final form, so that no matter which way it turns or which parts are exposed, the pattern will enrich those who encounter its beauty?

from the safe place in the bend of her arm and set her on the shelf. Later the doll was tucked away in the closet and finally relegated to a box of childhood treasures in the basement. A season had ended. Shelly had outgrown, left behind, and even forgotten (or so she thought) the childhood joy she had felt with Sweetypie cradled in the bend of her arm.

The past, the present, and the future, so close together, seem on occasion to be beyond reach of time.

We must let go of the past if we are to reach out to the unknown future with all its possibilities. For Shelly, it was in junior high that the excitement of the unknown became an ecstasy unexpected. She became a cheerleader. After one particularly exciting game finally won by her team, Shelly burst into the kitchen where her mom was waiting for her. "Oh, Mom!" Shelly exploded, jumping up and down, still filled with the excitement of the cheering crowd and the screaming thrill of victory. "Oh, Mom, it never gets better than this." Her mother, not wanting to be too casual about a moment so important to Shelly, smiled inwardly as she said tenderly, "Yes, Shelly, my dear, it does."

One season follows the next overnight, or so it seems. Years had flitted by, and the once excited cheerleader was now crowned high school homecoming queen. The cheering of the crowd was more personal this time. As Shelly rode in the parade, the people were calling her name. There was no mistaking the fact that the excitement was focused on her—it was even printed in the town paper. That night, when the shouting and the tumult had settled, Shelly sat on the bed by her mom and dad. "Oh, Mom," she said, her eyes alive with excitement, "oh, Mom, it never gets better than this!" Once again, with proper sensitivity to her young daughter's excitement, Shelly's mother responded, "Oh yes, my dear, it does."

Following more sunrises and sunsets, Shelly's tour to faraway places as a member of the Brigham Young University dance team brought applause that was translatable in every language. A postcard written home in a hurry exclaimed, "Mom and Dad, we are a real hit!" And then, perhaps remembering past times, but maybe not, Shelly scrawled a small postscript along the bottom of the card, "Mom, it never gets better than this," with a little smiley face to help carry the message. Her mom read the card and tucked it away to be used, perhaps, at some future date to confirm her answer not spoken, "Yes, Shelly, it does."

The bud must release its grasp if the flower is to bloom. With a sense of sacrifice, this young woman determined to leave the crowd and the applause and for eighteen months to fill a mission. Would it be worth it? she wondered. Could she ever come back to all of this? And yet she was drawn forward by a sense of purpose she did not fully understand at that time. From her mission in a far-off land, she wrote home regularly to report of the hard times and the good. Her parents watched for the letters with great anticipation. One day a letter came bearing a message across the top in bold strokes, "Oh, Mom and Dad, it never gets better than this." Pages of details followed about strangers who had become literally brothers and sisters in the gospel. Shelly loved them with a kind of love she had never experienced before. The sacrifice

The bud must release its grasp if the flower is to bloom.

she was making to serve her mission was a small thing to pay in exchange for this new kind of joy. There were no crowds, no cheering, not even any applause, but rather quiet testimony, tears of gratitude, and whispered expressions of love at the side of a baptismal font.

Another season and another time. In the temple on the glorious morning marked as her wedding day, while enveloped in her mother's arms, this little three-year-old who had so quickly blossomed now whispered in love and gratitude, "Oh, Mom, now I understand. It never gets better than this." Not wanting to lessen the joy of this grand experience, this event of eternal consequence, still her mother felt impelled to whisper, "Yes, my dear, it does."

Another year, in the quiet seclusion of a humble student apartment, it seemed that time stood still for a moment while generations looked on. A newborn babe nestled in that arm where Sweetypie had once claimed residence. As the baby took life nourishment from his mother's breast, his father expressed his own joy accompanying this drama, playing with great feeling a

Chopin sonata on the piano. The new grand-mother was on the scene to assist in this life-changing experience. Without taking her eyes from the miracle she held in her arms, and lacking adequate words to express her adoration and her joy, Shelly spoke in hushed tones, "Oh, Mom." Unable to restrain herself, her mother interrupted with words she had waited for years to confirm, "You are right, my dear, it never gets better than this."

Was she allowed for a brief moment to glimpse the future and see a stripling warrior in infancy?

One might wonder whether this elated grandmother's response was in reference to her daughter's joy or her own. Or was she allowed for a brief moment to glimpse the future and see a stripling warrior in infancy? Certainly a new grandmother witnessing the miracle of life and its continuation from one generation to another senses in an expanded way the joy of mother-hood. There was a consensus and complete agreement in that moment of lasting memory. Kneeling now at the side of the chair, and reaching out to mother and child, Shelly's mother in testimony reconfirmed, "It never gets better than this."

Baby Jake will grow day by day as his mother devotes herself to helping him increase "in wisdom and stature, and in favour with God and man" (Luke 2:52). The time will come, ever so quickly, when it might be said of him, "He will be a great missionary—he has so much of his dad in him." And so he will, but such an observation tells only part of the story. Those who would understand completely must comprehend the significant and far-reaching influence of his mother.

Has anyone ever read the inspiring account of Helaman's two thousand stripling warriors from the Book of Mormon without pondering the question, "What did their mothers know?" Of these young men we read, "Now they never had fought, yet they did not fear death; and they did think more upon the liberty of their fathers

Has anyone ever read the inspiring account of Helaman's two thousand stripling warriors from the Book of Mormon without pondering the question, "What did their mothers know?"

than they did upon their lives; yea, they had been taught by their mothers, that if they did not doubt, God would deliver them. And they rehearsed unto me the words of their mothers, saying: We do not doubt our mothers knew it" (Alma 56:47–48).

What did their mothers know? How did they teach in such a way that their testimony was absorbed into the fiber of their sons' souls, making them stripling warriors, courageous, bold, ready to fight, and determined to win? "Now this was the faith of these of whom I have spoken; they are young, and their minds are firm, and they do put their trust in God continually" (Alma 57:27).

Can one question the influence of Lucy Mack Smith, the Prophet Joseph's mother, in the life of her son? We read in Joseph's account of his first vision: "When the light had departed, I had no strength; but soon recovering in some degree, I went home. And as I leaned up to the fireplace, mother inquired what the matter was. I replied, 'Never mind, all is well—I am well enough off.' I then said to my mother, 'I have learned for myself that Presbyterianism is not true'" (Joseph Smith–History 1:20). It is noteworthy that following this experience of eternal significance for all mankind this young man "went home" and talked with his mother. She knew her son well enough to sense that something was the matter. She listened to him, believed him, and stood beside him throughout his life while he battled against the evil forces that opposed the restoration of the gospel.

In the three years that my husband, Heber, presided over the Canada Vancouver Mission, we were privileged to work with more than four hundred latter-day stripling warriors, young men and women determined to fight against the forces of evil. We were able to confirm over and over again the observation of President Ezra Taft Benson concerning this generation, "Never before on the face of this earth have the forces of evil and the forces of good been so well organized. . . . While our generation will be comparable in wickedness to the days of Noah, when the Lord cleansed the earth by flood, there is a major difference this time: God has saved for the final inning some of His stronger and most valiant children, who will help bear off the kingdom triumphantly." Then, speaking to the youth, he said, "You are the generation that must be prepared to meet your God" (*Ensign,* April 1987, p. 73).

On another occasion, President Benson told the young men and the young women of the Church, "You have been born at this time for a sacred and glorious purpose. It is not by chance that you have been reserved to come to earth in this last dispensation of the fulness of times. Your birth at this particular time was foreordained in the eternities. You are to be the royal army of the Lord in the last days. You are 'youth of the noble birthright.' (*Hymns,* 1985, no. 255.)" Speaking to the young men, he added: "In the spiritual battles you are waging, I see you as today's sons of Helaman. Remember well the Book of

"God has saved for the final inning some of His stronger and most valiant children, who will help bear off the kingdom triumphantly."

PRESIDENT EZRA
TAFT BENSON

15

Mormon account of Helaman's two thousand stripling warriors and how the teachings of their mothers gave them strength and faith. These marvelous mothers taught them to put on the whole armor of God, to place their trust in the Lord, and to doubt not. By so doing, not one of these young men was lost. (See Alma 53:10–23; 56:41–56.)" The stripling warriors of today, like those in times past, are strong largely because of what their mothers know and teach them, often without immediate evidence of the great lessons that are being woven into the fiber of their lives.

The stripling warriors of today, like those in times past, are strong largely because of what their mothers know and teach them.

With prophetic insight and concern for our time, President N. Eldon Tanner explained, "The war which was begun in heaven is raging here upon the earth; two great forces of right and wrong are pitted against each other. It is important that we fight for the right. We must have well trained, disciplined, fearless, and loyal volunteers well equipped with the proper weapons of war and with a determination to win." Mothers participating in the training of this great volunteer force might more fully understand their influence for good while considering the words of the Apostle Paul to young Timothy: "Call to remembrance the unfeigned faith that is in thee, which dwelt first in thy grandmother Lois, and thy mother Eunice; and I am persuaded that in thee also" (2 Timothy 1:5). Did this not give Timothy a sense of who he was: his identity, his heredity, his birthright as a man of faith, a man of God? Was he not profoundly influenced by his mother and grandmother, women of faith, women of God? Did they realize the sacred trust and great responsibility that was theirs when Timothy was only a child? Did they know the great missionary he was to become, and recognize their part in his preparation?

Once, in a zone conference, I stood to counsel with some young missionaries on a domestic matter. As I raised my voice and my finger, I began by saying, "Now, I may sound like your mother." A young man new to the mission spontaneously and wistfully blurted out, "Oh, I hope you do, I hope you do." I wondered how often he responded that way at home when his mother said, "Son, I have something I'd like to talk with you about." A likelier reaction might have been, "Oh, Mom, not again." Children may not always respond enthusiastically, but deep within they learn to listen to the messages of their mothers, messages that prepare them for the challenges they must face.

Did the mothers of the stripling warriors in the Book of Mormon teach their sons to polish their armor, cook their quail, mind their manners, eat proper food, shower every day, sew on buttons, have a proper haircut, and write home every week? Did they go with them to Mr. Mac's or some comparable first-century B.C. emporium to get new suits and shirts and socks and ties and luggage and send them off prepared for their missions? Those temporal, physical things can be accomplished in the last month or two—even week or two, if necessary—prior to departure for the battle. Such details, although

Children may not always respond enthusiastically, but deep within they learn to listen to the messages of their mothers, messages that prepare them for the challenges they must face.

18

important, pale in comparison to the importance of what stripling warriors learn from their mothers in preparation for the conflict.

The true preparation of a stripling warrior begins when a child is nestled in the arm of his or her mother, being nurtured physically and spiritually. As President Gordon B. Hinckley told the members of the Cottonwood Creek Stake in January 1995, "No calling in the Church can compare with being a father or mother in a family, and central to it all is mother. She knew the plan and the significance of it all." Mothers of stripling warriors sense the sacred role of motherhood and the eternal significance of every physical and spiritual experience that molds, shapes, refines, and prepares the body and the spirit of a child. This is not a Missionary Prep class to be taken in the late teenage years. It is a home-study course, and lessons often begin before daybreak and continue long after nightfall. Even though the course begins in the nursery, the time is ever so brief.

The true preparation of a stripling warrior begins when a child is nestled in the arm of his or her mother, being nurtured physically and spiritually.

There is so much to accomplish in so short a time, with so much opposition from the world in which we live, and so much at stake.

President Gordon B. Hinckley stated, "What a mother says to her children is not heard by the world, but it will be heard by posterity" (*Motherhood, A Heritage of Faith* [Salt Lake City: Deseret Book, 1995], p. 6). He further stated, "How grateful I am for mothers. I think it's been the mothers who have been the carriers and purveyors of faith throughout the history of the Church. I believe that with all my heart" (*Church News*, May 20, 1995). One mother and grandmother, Sister Linda Walker, was interviewed by a newspaper reporter in Canada who seemed bent on posing questions that would demean the role of motherhood. Reflecting on those questions, Sister Walker wrote a poem expressing how quickly the time had gone, and musing on the mixture of drudgery and joy it had been to raise a child. She acknowledged the opportunities for growth and

There is so much to accomplish in so short a time, with so much opposition from the world in which we live, and so much at stake.

self-expression that motherhood had offered her, and closed with this couplet:

> *You see, my day has been full*
> *of the precious and sublime*
> *Because of all this drudgery*
> *with this little soul of mine.*

Sunrise, sunset, and almost overnight this babe in the nursery is entering the Missionary Training Center, "well equipped with the proper weapons of war and with a determination to win." This is not to suggest by any means that the training is complete. It might be more accurate to say that the soil has been prepared. The time of sowing is past and maybe even forgotten in many respects. But every effort expended in those early years will in time be rewarded. A mother in her sacred trust is never left to sow alone. As the words of the hymn remind us:

Every effort expended in those early years will in time be rewarded.

> *Thou who knowest all our weakness,*
> *Leave us not to sow alone!*

Bid thine angels guard the furrows
Where the precious grain is sown,
Till the fields are crown'd with glory,
Filled with mellow, ripened ears,
Filled with fruit of life eternal
From the seed we sowed in tears.

(*Hymns,* no. 216)

Those tears come at different times, and for many different reasons. Only a mother knows the tears of anguish suffered when the welfare of her child is at stake.

The sacred mission of teaching and the ultimate joys that attend—those most lasting, those felt most deeply—are often born out of struggle, anxiety, and determination that is sustained only through unwavering faith in God. The moments of greatest anxiety can become forerunners to the deepest joy and ultimate ecstasy when a mother teaches her child.

One mother, Ruth Yancey, tells of the anxiety she felt in her responsibility to teach her young son, Steven. A few days after Steven's birth, Sister Yancey became aware that heavy doses of oxygen administered to save her son's life had caused the blood vessels in his eyes to rupture. He was blind. One morning after her husband had gone to work, Sister Yancey cradled her son close to her and began pleading with the Lord. "Help me to know how to teach him, what to say, how to show him so he can accomplish each task," she prayed. "Inspire me because I am your tool in teaching this special spirit. I'm weak. I'm uneducated. I'm unknowledgeable about what should be done. Help me to know what to do and how Steven and I can accomplish it." This faithful mother's prayer could be the pleadings of every mother until her child is ready to be released from her arms to the service of the Lord, where the growth will continue.

The moments of greatest anxiety can become forerunners to the deepest joy and ultimate ecstasy when a mother teaches her child.

The mother of one of our missionaries, who for nineteen years anticipated that day when she would take her son to the Missionary Training Center, trusting the Lord to watch over him, felt that he was ready and that she must be willing to let him go. This mother, Diane Pullan Fehr, shared with me the lines she had penned conveying her feelings on that eventful day at the MTC:

As we went through the MTC doors,
I said, "Heavenly Father, he is yours."
With tears burning in my eyes
We said our farewells and good-byes.
He's not off to kindergarten, he's not out to play,
He's doing the Lord's work today.
I guess the mailbox will become our best friend
As we wait for the letters he will send.
A strange silence fell on our home.
Someone is missing and I feel alone.
No "Hey, Mom," or even his voice on the phone.
The basketball is still in the hall.
I see his smiling photo on the wall.
His winter coat is hanging on the rack.
It will be two years until he is back.
Too much milk in the fridge, no more wash to do.
My work load is lightening, but, Son, I miss you.
Crying, I walk into his room.
Then I remember Christ's empty tomb.
My sacrifice is so small

Compared to it all.
Christ bled and died for me;
I will not act selfishly.
Bitter sweet, the words repeat,
"Feed my sheep, it's time to reap.
The fields are white as snow—
Let your boy go."
At the airport it is time to board.
He is so eager to serve the Lord.
It is hard to let go of my boy's hand,
For when he returns, he will be a man.
I look at this missionary with testimony strong—
Yesteryears, where have they gone?
Memories run through my mind back in time
Of his childhood, when he was mine.
I would hug him and read him a nursery rhyme,
That little boy with a toothless grin.
Oh, my heart did he win.
For all the memories, Christmas and such,
It's been great, Lord, I thank you so much.
Rites of passage, children at play,
I carefully close the door on yesterday.
Remember, write us, keep in touch,
For we love you very much.

Last departure call
Echoes off the concourse wall.
It's time to go, hurry, run,
Good-bye, my son.
Silver airplane with wings so wide,
With our precious boy inside.
He is onward to that strange new land
With a Book of Mormon in his hand.
Only boys, these missionaries that preach,
But think how many souls they reach.
Father, I'm proud as I can be
That he chose to follow Thee.
And as I turn and walk away,
"God bless our boy," I silently pray.
Into the bright light through the airport doors
And once again, Father, I know he is yours.

As mothers said good-bye at the MTC, I was there to welcome their sons and daughters into the mission field. How often I wished to have just a few minutes with each missionary's mother. I wanted to say, "Tell me about this boy or girl, this stripling warrior who is willing to go in to battle on the Lord's side and fight for the right, not with a sword but with the word of God. Tell me, who is this missionary, really?"

My husband and I would observe them day after day, some of them homesick and discouraged and yet determined to carry on. On many occasions our experiences with these young men and women would echo those of Helaman and his stripling warriors, "never had [we] seen so great courage" (Alma 56:45). Since it was not possible to talk to their mothers about their experiences that spanned from the nursery to the mission field, I determined that I might learn about what their mothers taught them by talking with these latter-day stripling warriors themselves. As time would permit without interfering with their missionary labors, I made inquiries and, with the missionaries' approval, recorded their responses. The comments of these young men and women soon led me to feel that their mothers were worthy of commendation even like that accorded the mothers of the stripling warriors in the Book of Mormon. Our days are different, but motherhood knows no bounds.

The tender responses from these missionaries

give evidence that a mother's years of love and concern are recorded not in journals but, as Paul taught, "in fleshy tables of the heart" (2 Corinthians 3:3). These young missionaries seemed to sense—maybe some of them for the first time—the profound influence of what they had been taught by lecture, by love, by preachment, and by practice, by women who gave their time and their lives to the work of motherhood.

Our days are different, but motherhood knows no bounds.

On one occasion when I was expressing my love for these young men and women, I told them I didn't know how their mothers could stand to let them leave home in the first place, because it was so hard for me to see them leave the mission field. One said, with an understanding smile, "But you didn't raise us when we were teenagers." Growth is a process, often trying if not downright painful for both parents and youth. How rewarding it is to finally recognize the multitude of priceless lessons that have been internalized by young people and their parents as well, often without their even realizing it at the time!

In a zone conference, one strong-willed young man stood with conviction and spoke persuasively of diligence and obedience. When I complimented him privately on his presentation, he rolled his eyes and said, "My mom would never believe this." I sensed there had perhaps been a change in his attitude or his heart, in his conduct or his understanding. He was like a blossom unfolding, maturing in a marvelous way because of the seeds planted years before. Yes, I think his mother would have believed it. Mothers see far beyond the evidence of immaturity, messy rooms, poor grades, and, sometimes, wrong choices. They see their sons and daughters not as they are, but as they are becoming.

Mothers see their sons and daughters not as they are, but as they are becoming.

As Heber and I examined the process of their becoming, we learned that today's stripling warriors feel secure when they have specific guidelines, rules, policies. They want someone to follow up and reinforce their confidence, to reassure them that they're doing well. We learned that sometimes they need to suffer the consequences of wrong choices and learn—often painfully—from their mistakes, knowing all the while that love and acceptance are uncondi-tional. We learned that they need reminders during the early stages of bad habits they might be forming, and that they need encouragement and direc-tion by example. It is important to praise in public and counsel in pri-vate, and to help them understand the difference between sin and error. We learned that stripling warriors have fears that are real. Their responses of support and loyalty seemed strength-ened when we acknowledged some of our own feelings of inadequacy and dependence on the Lord. Working with these young men and women, we learned that genuine love and understanding, combined with clearly defined, consistent boundaries (not barriers), will build bonds of relationships as strong as steel. We learned that the making of a man or woman begins in a mother's arms and at a mother's knee.

Genuine love and understanding, combined with clearly defined, consistent boundaries (not barriers), will build bonds of relationships as strong as steel.

Each mother with her own unique, customized curriculum is helping to prepare a mighty army. To suppose that nurturing, tutoring, and mothering should be the same for all children is folly. A fable tells of some animals who organized a school. To make it easier to administer the curriculum and evaluate progress, every animal was to take the same subjects. According to the fable, the rabbits started at the top of the class in running but had a nervous breakdown because of makeup work in swimming. The eagle was a problem child and was disciplined severely. In the climbing class, he beat others to the top of the tree, but he insisted on getting there his own way. The prairie dog stayed out of school because the administration would not add digging and burrowing to the curriculum. The very skills and gifts that made each one great individually were being overlooked through a curriculum designed for blanket application to everyone.

I emphasize this point because the questions that I asked the missionaries were not intended to solicit answers suggesting that there is only one parenting curriculum for everyone. Rather, I hoped to identify a few basic principles that are at the foundation, the very core of what is essential for the preparation of these stripling warriors.

In statements that the prophets of the Church have made over the years concerning their mothers, there are many parallels with the thoughts expressed by missionaries today. Their candid responses to my questions have been more profound, tender, and revealing than I could have imagined. They verify that there are mothers today who know what earlier mothers knew and are true to the sacred trust that is theirs. In all the interviews, I felt the missionaries' deep love and gratitude, evidenced often by tender emotions and sometimes tears as these young men and women spoke of the influence of their mothers. It was as though for many this was a new discovery, something they had not realized before. I would often inquire, "Have you shared these feelings of love with your mother?" A nod of the head and a countenance of reflection would usually confirm that these thoughts had not been shared. Listening to the missionaries' expressions of gratitude and love, I realized that these beautiful tributes to mothers were not mine to keep but rather to share. After transcribing many of their comments, I would often send a copy to the surprised but grateful mother.

In all of the visits, questions, and conversations I had with our missionaries, no one, not one, spoke of the fancy clothes his or her mother wore. They didn't remember the perfect color coordination of the furniture in the home. They never spoke of their mothers' social status, title, or position. They didn't remember their moms' imperfections or mistakes. The things they remembered confirm that the molding of a stripling warrior today, as in times past, begins very early in a child's life through the profound influence of a mother. Events that at the time may appear insignificant may in a later season emerge as moments of lasting impact. In the words of Emily Dickinson, "Sometimes when I consider the tremendous consequences from little things . . . a chance word . . . a tap on the shoulder or a wink of an

Events that at the time may appear insignificant may in a later season emerge as moments of lasting impact.

eye, I am tempted to think there are no little things."

The first of my interviews was with a young elder who was spiritually mature beyond his years. I asked, "What comes to your mind when you think of your mother?" He thought for a moment and then smiled. "One thing I remember clearly," he said. "When I was a baby and just learning to walk, I bumped my head on the corner of the TV and I remember her holding me."

Considering all the lessons that might have been taught over twenty years in various settings and circumstances, this response was quite surprising and made me curious. "That's remarkable," I said. "That would have been almost twenty years ago. What is it that you remember about that?" I expected some detailed report of major consequence.

"Just that she held me," he whispered, with tears filling his eyes.

Do you think that tender illustration carried by a young man into the mission field twenty years later was ever recorded on the ledger of his mother as being a significant event? How many other such incidents in the molding and shaping of these stripling warriors are overlooked by mothers who may feel they don't measure up? Labors that may seem incidental are of eternal consequence. The Lord tells us, "I will encircle thee in the arms of my love" (D&C 6:20). That feeling of being encircled with love was familiar to that young man because of the tender care of his mother, who was there and who held him in her arms when it mattered so much.

One elder explained with a smile his mother's method of getting the children to sleep at night. "She always sang a song with just one word: 'there.' That would put us to sleep. Just holding me in her arms and patting me, saying, 'There, there, there, there,' made me know that she loved me." Keep in mind that this is the memory of a twenty-one-year-old man. Do little things matter? Do they leave an impression? Do they say more than we might ever know?

I asked another particularly mature nineteen-year-old if he remembered a spiritual experience he had had with his mother that he felt comfortable sharing. He thought for a minute, then with a warm smile related: "We'd just jump in the car to go for a milk run at night. My mom would say, 'We're out of milk; we've got to have it for tomorrow morning,' and she would ask me to go with her. We'd go and just talk." This elder was from a large family, and the feeling he remembered just from being alone with his mother was recorded in his mind as a spiritual experience.

The feeling he remembered just from being alone with his mother was recorded in his mind as a spiritual experience.

One question I liked to ask the missionaries was, "When you think of your home, which is your favorite room?" I was especially touched by one sister's response: "Whenever I walked into the house, I would always holler, 'Mom!' That would be the first thing I would say. All of us kids would. Wherever Mom was, that was my favorite room. That was where I usually went. I didn't always say anything, but I always went to that place, at least for a minute." Is it possible that such a profound lesson went unreported on that mother's list of pluses and minuses as she evaluated her effectiveness? Was she ever aware that the favorite room in the house was where she was, whatever room that may have been? Would it have made a difference if she weren't there?

Mother Teresa of Calcutta shares a story about the influence of a mother's presence: "The home is where the mother is. Once I found a child on the streets. I took him to our children's home and gave him a bath and some clean clothes, but he ran away. He was found again by somebody else, but he ran away a second time. After we found him, I said to the sisters, 'Please follow that child and see where he goes when he runs away.'

Was she ever aware that the favorite room in the house was where she was, whatever room that may have been?

"When the child ran away a third time they followed him, and there, under a tree, was his mother. She had put stones under a small earthenware vessel and was cooking some food she had found. The sister asked the child, 'Why did you run away from the home?' And the child answered, 'But this is my home because this is where my mother is.'" (Kathryn Spink, *Life in the Spirit* (New York: Harper and Row, 1983).

Most of the missionaries spoke of family home evenings, family vacations and celebrations, family traditions, family prayer and scripture study, and other activities recognized as contributing to strong families. They were the beneficiaries of such rich experiences. There is no way to put a price on the blessing it is for a young man or woman to be nurtured in a home with a mother and a father who love each other, love the Lord, and teach their children by precept and example. But there were mothers whose circumstances made it very difficult to provide some of those traditional safeguards, yet they still achieved remarkable success. One elder who had the reputation throughout the entire mission of being obedient in attitude and conduct explained, "We've had some rough times. We went through a divorce when I was eight. My mom was on her own with six kids, but she went to church every week. I can't remember a time that she didn't take us. Even when times were tough, she always loaded us up in the van and took us to church."

"Was that hard?" I asked.

"I always felt the security of my mom when I

stayed with her, and I knew she'd raise me right."
He paused, and then as if he had just discovered
a new truth he said with conviction, "That's why
I'm here today."

"In what ways is her influence affecting you
today?"

He spoke in a tone of deep gratitude. "In my
patriarchal blessing it says that the faith of my
mother will be an example to me in the eternities." There was no question that that blessing
was not just for a future time, but was already
evident in his young years. His name wasn't
Timothy, and his mother wasn't named Eunice,
but the blessings of the inheritance of faith from a
faithful mother were his. Those same blessings
are available to people in every generation who
are fortunate to have faithful mothers and grand-
mothers.

Surely all mothers want to offer "ideal" homes
to their children, and many feel that they have
fallen short when those ideals fail to materialize.
They might take heart from one missionary's
assessment of his mother: "She takes a problem
and totally turns it around to make you look at it

from a different point of view. 'Don't bring good news to me,' she always says. 'I like problems. Problems strengthen me.'" A stripling warrior can gain much strength from the courage his mother shows in less-than-ideal circumstances.

A stripling warrior can gain much strength from the courage his mother shows.

"What comes to your mind when you think of your mom?" I asked another young elder.

"When I think of my mom," he replied, "I think of the Savior and his example. Even though she is inactive, she exemplifies the Savior in the way that she loves. She loves so unselfishly. She's proud of me and thinks it's great that I'm on a mission. She supports me. She writes to me. She loves me."

The Lord said, "By this shall all men know that ye are my disciples, if ye have love one to another" (John 13:35). This mother has the attribute of a disciple, and passed that great attribute of love on to her son. His love for people, all people, was evident as he taught and loved unconditionally. His weekly letters expressed his love for his mother and for the Lord.

I spoke with a young elder who was very effective in his missionary labors. He was confident, enthusiastic, and eager. This led me to suppose that his home situation must have been ideal. "Elder," I asked, sitting across the table with a small recorder in my hand, "what first comes to your mind when you think of your mom?"

He looked off into space for a moment, as if sifting through nineteen years of happenings to find some singular experience that might emerge above all the rest. "Well," he said, "I remember one thing." I waited eagerly to learn what that one thing might be. "I don't know why this comes to mind," he said, "but when I was young, she had to work two jobs, so she taught dancing some days. When she'd be down teaching, I would clean the kitchen. I remember one day she came up from a long day of teaching dancing. I was still cleaning the kitchen. We started singing together, 'Let Us All Press On,' and that's just a real fun memory." Then, in a serious tone, he declared with conviction, "I knew then that my mom would press on."

It is quite possible that his mother never

quoted the scripture, "Wherefore, ye must press forward with a steadfastness in Christ, having a perfect brightness of hope, and a love of God and of all men" (2 Nephi 31:20), but she believed it, lived it, and passed it on to her son. This elder was known for his relentless effort to press forward through many challenges. I never saw him without a smile on his face. He seemed to possess "a perfect brightness of hope."

With this elder's permission, I sent a copy of the questions and his responses to his mother. She wrote back, "I have posted the letter on our bulletin board and read it often. It will have a special spot in our missionary scrapbook, but probably not until I have memorized it." Do you think she ever realized how singing a simple song could teach such a profound lesson? There must have been many times when she felt concern that she was not doing all she should or could to be a perfect mom. I learned that her situation was actually not what one would consider ideal, yet the results of her faithful mothering were profound. She wrote:

"At times life has seemed discouraging. It has

not been what I expected as I kept the commandments and remained faithful to my covenants. I have laughed and said that the Lord lost my list of expected blessings and replaced it with one of his own. The blessings are not what I expected, but they are certainly precious. At one point right after I found myself divorced I wondered how I could pass on the testimony of temple marriage to my children. I was feeling cheated and couldn't see what my temple marriage had done for me. I had temporarily lost the eternal view of my sealings. Then it all hit me: my temple sealing was precious. It continues to bind my family together. If I continue to live worthy, it still seals me to my children and will some day seal me to a worthy companion.

"I began to realize that the Lord's list of blessings wasn't that different from my own. The most important blessing was at the top of both lists, the blessings of eternal life and exaltation with my family. My temple covenants will always bind my children to me. That kept me going. I knew that no trials in this earth would be too much if I stayed on track to return to my Heavenly Father and taught my children the way back. I would be ungrateful to deny his hand in blessing me.

Sixteen years ago as I faced the difficult task of raising four children alone, I wondered how I could do it. I'm grateful that I have the gospel of Jesus Christ. With God's help, anything is possible."

This struggling single mother raised her son to become a stripling warrior. She taught him to never give up. He said he had learned that with God's help nothing was impossible—a profound lesson from a mother who undoubtedly anguished at times over feelings of failure.

Many mothers confess feelings of inadequacy at times, especially when they listen to Mother's Day talks expounding the virtues of seemingly tireless, totally selfless, apparently saintly mothers. How surprised they might be to realize what a difference simple, little things make in a child's life. Those little things were the first to be recalled to mind by many of our missionaries.

"I knew that no trials in this earth would be too much if I stayed on track to return to my Heavenly Father and taught my children the way back."

"My favorite time was in the summer around seven o'clock," recalled one elder. "We would all go out and sit on a big wood swing we have and just talk. To me, that was like my favorite thing in the world to do, just to go out and sit on the back patio and talk at night with my family." When I asked about the nature of their conversations, he couldn't remember specifically. "Just things," he said, "but I remember how I felt." Sweet memories are often made in simple ways.

Another elder remembered with fondness, "When we were camping, Mom would never forget to enjoy a sunset, and she always marveled at the beautiful flowers. One of my favorite memories of her is her ability to enjoy the beauties of nature as we were walking along the trail. Once there was some Indian paintbrush that was all different colors, and she decided to collect a variety of shades. In the end she had a huge bouquet of Indian paintbrush, going from pale yellow all the way through deep red, with each exact shade there in order. She was just happy as she walked along that little trail and observed the beauty of nature and the works of God. She taught me to enjoy those same things. I'm able to respect our Father in Heaven and his love, and to appreciate the power and majesty that he has in his hand. My mom taught me that."

"Did you realize that your mother was teaching you that when she was picking the paintbrush along the way?" I asked.

"No, I certainly didn't," he replied. "I didn't realize that I had learned all these lessons in such subtle ways."

A young man from a family of eight children remembered that it was sometimes difficult to get individual attention. "But," he said, "whenever I was feeling discouraged or I needed a little bit of support, I would find some treats or something tucked away especially for me. I can remember one day I came home after a difficult day at school and went down to my bedroom and there was a plate of cookies and a note from my mother. I will never forget that. It was such a surprise to go in there and be able to read that note and feel of her love for me. She was able to do that every time that I needed her. She would always take the time to talk with me. With eight children, she couldn't give me all of her attention, but she knew when I needed it." How many times do weary mothers set aside their own needs to be there for their children?

Do little things matter? It may be years before their true worth is realized. But, as the Lord counsels, "Be not weary in well-doing, for . . . out of small things proceedeth that which is great" (D&C 64:33).

I was profoundly impressed by one "little thing" that I observed when Heber and I attended stake conferences in the far northern part of the province. During our three years in the mission we attended twice each year, making six conferences in all. Following that first conference, etched into my mind and heart was the memory of a young family sitting on the front row. They came from some distance to be there; they lived in the village of Horsefly, beyond One Hundred Mile House, in a very small branch of the Church. Mother and father, three older brothers, one older sister, and one young boy, about ten years of age, sang with enthusiasm, "We Thank Thee, O God, for a Prophet." It seemed as though they were a small chorus by themselves, all watching the chorister as if they had been trained, with the entire congregation accompanying them. One of the older boys stood holding the hymnbook in both hands, with his arms wrapped like parentheses around his younger brother standing in front of him.

During the conference, each member of the family appeared to be hanging on every word spoken, as if they had come with a bucket to be filled. Occasionally some interaction between an older brother and the younger boy revealed the closeness of their relationship.

Each member of the family appeared to be hanging on every word spoken, as if they had come with a bucket to be filled.

The mother was wearing a red silk dress. But it was not the dress that initially caught my attention; it was her expression of joyful abundance as she leaned forward occasionally to look over her family, as if to be reassured of her wealth. Every child was in place, responsive to all that was going on.

Six months later, the same events were

48

repeated, with only minor changes. Some of the family members wore new clothes to accommodate their growing years, but the mother was still attired in her red silk dress.

Over the course of three years, young men and women show signs of growth and change. And yet, some things remain the same. Each time we attended stake conference, we eagerly looked forward to seeing this family in their places on the front row. Each time, the faithful mother wore the same red silk dress. It always looked nice, almost new, as if it were simply resistant to wear. The dress was becoming a symbol to me of selfless sacrifice, eternal priorities, and an understanding of lasting values.

The dress was becoming a symbol to me of selfless sacrifice, eternal priorities, and an understanding of lasting values.

The last conference we were to attend with the Saints in that distant area, we anxiously anticipated what we had come to consider a vital part of the conference. I found myself hoping that the sermon that had become so vivid in my mind and heart each conference relating to humility, spirituality, and seeking first the kingdom of God would not be interrupted or lessened. I wanted to come home remembering always the unspoken sermon, the lesson I had learned at that stake conference. I looked anxiously for the mother in her red silk dress.

Finally the family arrived, taking their place on the front row. The eldest boy, now nineteen years of age, wore a new suit, white shirt, and tie. The younger brothers had new shirts and pants. Their sister's stylish, youthful dress was obviously a recent purchase; she wore it with a wonderful smile of satisfaction and joy. Mom and Dad were in their usual places, anchors to the family. There was the eldest son, prepared to leave for his mission. He was ready to launch out into the world of service to the Lord. His mother sat there in her red silk dress, her face reflecting her inexpressible joy. The sermon was complete, the message delivered, the events recorded.

Now, if that boy were asked after arriving in the mission field, "What comes to your mind when you think of your mom?" it is hard to imagine him saying, "She had one silk dress and wore it every Sunday." But it is very possible that what that dress symbolized will never be forgotten.

On one occasion President Brigham Young wrote of his mother, Abigail (Nabby) Howe Young, "She was . . . frugal: she carefully preserved her one silk dress to wear throughout her life" (Leonard J. Arrington and Susan Arrington Madsen, *Mothers of the Prophets* [Salt Lake City: Deseret Book, 1987], p. 30). Do you suppose the mother from Horsefly, Canada, knew she was mirroring the experience of a prophet's mother in her own actions? The example of faithful families is profound in every generation.

Because they had prayed and studied the scriptures with their family, two young friends of mine, Angela and her brother William, were prepared to turn to their Father in Heaven when they needed help. Home alone for the day, they were responsible for milking the family cow. By the time the job was half done, the cow was jumpy and starting to kick. William sent Angela to call the neighbor for help. She writes:

"I went up to the house and had a wonderful thought come into my mind. I was to call home, my Heavenly Father, so I shut the door and knelt down to pray. I asked Heavenly Father to help Daisy to be still and not kick so we could finish milking.

"I went back out the door, went down to the pen, and climbed over the fence. William asked if he [the neighbor] was coming. I told him no. William asked why, and I replied, 'Because I didn't call him. I called Heavenly Father.' I told William that He would help us if we had faith. William sat on the stump and watched me. At first I was a little scared. I said a silent prayer, and she didn't kick."

Children learn to pray first by repeating a few simple words after their parents. Lucky indeed is the child who learns about Heavenly Father in his or her youth by participating in family prayers and family scripture study. Angela's letter continues:

"Dad and Mom also told us to stay home. We weren't allowed to go play at the neighbors'. It was very tempting because they had just gotten a new trampoline. They called over several times, but we said no. One time William almost went over. He had on his shoes and his coat and was outside. He sat on the fence for about five minutes, then he came inside. It was very tempting to disobey Mom and Dad, but we hung in there.

"When I told Mom and Dad at the supper table today, Dad said that I could relate this story to the iron rod story. The reason it was hard to stay home was because they kept asking us to come and play, just like the big and spacious building when they are teasing and making fun of the people that are clinging to the rod. They were calling for the righteous to join the wicked. Well, it's similar to our experience. I felt really blessed. I felt the Spirit."

She could testify concerning what it meant to understand and follow the guidelines she learned from reading the Book of Mormon in her family circle.

Angela in her tender years was bearing testimony of the things she had experimented upon and had come to know. She could testify concerning what it meant to understand and follow the guidelines she learned from reading the Book of Mormon in her family circle. Angela and William are stripling warriors in training.

One young mother expressed her feelings and testimony regarding scripture reading with her children:

"A couple of weeks ago I was reading the Book of Mormon to our youngest son, David, at bedtime. David is seven years old. We were reading about Nephi's vision of the tree of life and all the attendant symbols and interpretations. David was concerned about the river of filthy waters. He didn't want to drown in it, so he said to me, 'I'm holding on to the iron rod, right?' I assured him that he was. Then he remembered his little school friend and added, 'What if I saw Jonathan in the water and I reached out my hand?' David wasn't content to save himself. He wanted to save his friend, too."

We must not underestimate our children's ability to respond to the scriptures.

We must not underestimate our children's ability to respond to the scriptures. We do not always have to feed them a watered-down storybook or animated version of the Bible or Book of Mormon. The language of scriptures has a power and majesty all its own. David's mother tells another story:

"Fifteen years ago, when our oldest son, Spencer, was only four years old, I was sitting on his bed one night reading to him. When we got to the part where the newly resurrected Savior was speaking to Mary in the garden, a holy feeling came into the room. I read the part where Mary finally recognizes the Savior and says, 'Master.' Spencer pulled the blanket over his head to hide his tears. He had been touched by the Spirit and it had brought tears to his eyes. When our children are young, still 'trailing clouds of glory' from God, as Wordsworth wrote, they are the most teachable. We must not let the moment pass."

But how is this teaching accomplished? This faithful mother continues:

"It isn't easy to set up new programs and routines in our families, especially if the children are older. They may balk, they may complain; but if parents are consistent over a period of time they will discover that their children have settled into the routine. Over the years my husband and I have attempted many approaches to family scripture study. When about six months ago we told our children we would be reading the scriptures at the table right before supper, they did not receive the news with gladness. Six of our seven children are boys, and food is very important to them. 'That's a bad idea, Dad. That time won't work. Everybody will be too hungry. The food will get cold. We already read that in seminary. I'm reading that on my own.'

"But now, when I set the table for supper, I put a Book of Mormon on everyone's plate. Our son Steven, who is our appointed scripture policeman, tells us where we are reading and we all open our books. The routine has become established."

President Joseph Fielding Smith said of his mother, "I used to sit . . . as a little child and listen to her stories about the pioneers. . . . She used to teach me and put in my hands, when I was old enough to read, things that I could understand. . . . I had a mother who saw to it that I did read, and I loved to read" (Arrington and Madsen, *Mothers of the Prophets,* p. 151). Children whose appetites are trained for good books will learn to love books. If the routine of reading scriptures and other uplifting books is established, they will be comfortable feasting upon the words of Christ, which will tell them all the things they should do (see 2 Nephi 32:3).

One missionary remembered his mother's "yellow book of stories about pioneers. She would sit in the hallway upstairs so that we could hear her in our rooms, reading these stories of pioneers. I thought it was pretty neat."

Children whose appetites are trained for good books will learn to love books.

"Did your mother ever read to you?" I asked another elder, a former linebacker on a football team.

"All the time," he said. "We always had a story right before bedtime."

"Were there any particular stories you liked?" I asked.

"Yes," he responded quickly, "*The Three Little Pigs.*"

"What was it you liked about that story?"

"The persistence of the wolf."

This young man stood in the park one day and testified with persistence regarding the truthfulness of the Book of Mormon, silencing contenders with the strength of his spirit. When were the seeds for such persistence planted? Might that quality have been awakened within him as a child, maybe even by the tone of his mother's voice when she read stories?

One elder remembered being read to and then in turn seeing his mother read to his younger brother and sister. "She read parts of her journal to us, about when we were little kids. And Dr. Seuss books—*The Cat in the Hat* or whatever. When you grow up and you have a little brother and see your mom read to him, you know she thinks it's important to have time for the children. It shows that she cares."

Consider the hundreds of little things mothers do every day, evidence that they care. Are not such efforts, small though they may seem, the foundation stones upon which character is built? One sister missionary remembered spending hours planting flowers in the garden with her mother, "helping to beautify the world around us." That wise mother was planting more than flowers; she was planting memories that would bear fruit of eternal worth.

Many ideas that mothers plant come in the form of "one-liners" that their children never forget. The missionaries often got a chuckle out of remembering some of their mothers' famous sayings, and would repeat them when asked, with the same tone and emphasis as they remembered their mothers using. Some of those one-liners were brief sermons in themselves:

"Be home on time."

"Now remember, I love you."

"Because I'm the mother, that's why."

"We're making memories."

"You can do it."

"Remember, Son, in the preexistence you chose to come to this family."

"This too shall pass."

"Remember you're special; you are one of Heavenly Father's favorites."

"Two wrongs don't make a right."

"After you've done all you can, then wait for what God wants you to do." (This was a loose translation of a Japanese saying an elder remembered his mother always using.)

A powerful "one-liner" in one sister mission-

Did her mother know when she placed that little sign over the door years before that its simple message would become a beacon light, a commitment her daughter would make to return home with honor?

ary's life was hung as a visual reminder in her home. "We have a brass plate hung on our door: Return with Honor. Every time we leave the house it just subliminally goes into the back of your head. It's the neatest thing. I love it."

"How has that affected your mission?" I asked.

"I'm going to return with honor for sure," she said with conviction. This sister became a powerful influence for good in every situation. She was totally committed, as though in each decision she anticipated that day when she would return and report on her labors. Did her mother know when she placed that little sign over the door years before that its simple message would become a beacon light, a commitment her daughter would make to return home with honor?

"Did you have rules in your family?" I asked a young man who always

60

wore a big smile to match his delightful sense of humor. "Yes," he said, nodding his head and rolling his eyes. "We had to listen to our mother. Our mother taught and trained us, and our mother had the final word. So that was basically it. We had to listen to Mom or suffer the consequences."

President George Albert Smith wrote of his mother, "She was a strict disciplinarian, and we always knew that when she told us to do anything she meant it" (Arrington and Madsen, *Mothers of the Prophets,* p. 123). Few mothers will ever have the task of rearing a prophet of God, and those who do will likely not recognize it at the time. But every mother can know that her son or daughter is a god in embryo, with an eternal destiny far surpassing any earthly calling. The labor of motherhood is eternal in nature, and the consequences affect generations past, present, and future.

Every mother can know that her son or daughter is a god in embryo, with an eternal destiny far surpassing any earthly calling.

Another elder remembers his mother's method of enforcing the family rules. "One particular time that I can remember was when I was throwing fruit at cars. A man stopped his car and came and told what I had done. I thought I was in for it. My mom just took me inside and sat me on the bed and talked to me. Then she just left and made me sit there and think about it for quite a while. It was better than any punishment that she could have given."

"Can you think of a specific time when your mother corrected you and you didn't like it?" I asked one young man.

"Yes," he laughed. "It's when I make a promise. She does this to kind of irritate me so I make sure to keep my promises. Every time I'd make one she'd say, 'A promise is a sacred thing, do not haste to make it. For once a promise has been made, you must be sure to keep it.'" His sing-song manner as he rolled his eyes and performed hand motions told me that that message had been repeated a few times. This missionary worked in the office for a short time. When he was transferred out, the office staff petitioned the mission president to leave him there, saying he was so dependable and so much fun.

The effects of loving discipline are far reaching. "It seems like everything my mom did was to help us," said one elder. "With six children we always had activities we were involved in. She was always trying to push us to make us better people in all things, not just in sports but in school and music, too. She made me play the piano. That was one of the things I really didn't want to do. There were times I had to get a paper typed and she'd stay up until midnight and help me type the paper. I'd read it off and she'd type it up." This strong, sturdy, broad-shouldered young man spoke tenderly of his feelings for his mom.

"What do you think is the most significant influence your mother has had on your spiritual development?" I asked him.

"I think seeing her bear her testimony in church," he answered. "Sometimes, when the weather was so bad we couldn't get to church, we would hold our meeting in our living room. We'd sing hymns and bear testimony to each other. That was one of the experiences I felt was really neat."

"Do you remember a specific spiritual time

with your family that you would feel comfortable sharing?" I asked another elder.

"Yeah," he responded. "We always knelt around the table and blessed the kids who were away at college. It's amazing to think that now I'm out on a mission, everyone still gathers every evening and probably mentions me in their prayers." He dropped his head, and when he looked up I felt that for just a moment he had returned in his heart to that family circle and felt enveloped by their presence and their love.

"It's amazing to think that now I'm out on a mission, everyone still gathers every evening and probably mentions me in their prayers."

The power of a mother's prayers should never be underestimated. President Heber J. Grant said of his mother, "So near to the Lord would she get in her prayers that they were a wonderful inspiration to me from childhood to manhood" (Arrington and Madsen, *Mothers of the Prophets,* p. 109). President Ezra Taft Benson explained his feelings, "When your mother prays with such fervor, night after night, you think twice before you do something to disappoint her" (Ibid., p. 197). One of our elders said, "When I came on my mission, I saw a statue of a lady kneeling and praying. I've never forgotten that. I know that my mom has been on her knees every day for me." He did not doubt his mother knew her Father in Heaven!

"I think one of the most spiritual experiences I've had with my mom would be at my farewell," another elder volunteered. "My mom doesn't have too much confidence in speaking publicly, but she is very gifted in singing. She sang 'I Heard Him Come' and 'I Walked Today Where Jesus Walked' at my farewell. The Spirit was so strong, there was no doubt that she knew what she was singing." Through his mother's testimony in song, he remembered "one of the most spiritual experiences I've had." When mothers provide opportunities for their children to recognize the feelings of the Spirit, they are preparing those children to become stripling warriors.

Being with his mother in the temple was a spiritual high point for another elder. "I will always remember waiting for her in the celestial room. I was reflecting upon the meaning of things, and I just felt a great urgency to see her. I remember when she came into the room, I embraced my mother and cried tears of joy for such a wonderful person in my life and such a great teacher." What a glorious experience that must have been, not just for the missionary, but for his faithful mother! That rich harvest was a fitting climax to the long seasons of planting, tending, nurturing, pruning, and nourishing both physically and spiritually.

"Elder," I asked another young man, one who had demonstrated unusual leadership and self-discipline and confidence, "what characteristics does your mother have that you will look for in an eternal companion?" This question always brought a smile from the missionaries (as though they were surprised that I thought the idea of an eternal companion ever crossed their minds in the mission field).

Without hesitation he responded, "Loyalty. My mom is very loyal to my dad. She values his judgment and his opinion."

His answer brought to mind a statement

concerning George Washington's home and his mother: "Perhaps the most important factor of this fine home was Mary's cheerful acceptance of her husband's leadership. . . . Not only did she do her part to create a happy home, she also made it possible for George to develop complete faith in his father. It is difficult to overestimate the value of this gift of complete trust. . . . As a consequence George matured more rapidly than the average child" (William H. Wilbur, *The Making of George Washington* [Clayton Printers, 1973], pp. 44–45).

We read in Proverbs of such a woman, "The heart of her husband doth safely trust in her, so that he shall have no need of spoil" (Proverbs 31:11). The elder who spoke of loyalty was absolutely loyal and unwavering in his missionary labors. He could be sent anywhere in the mission with complete trust. Did his mother realize the value of the model she was providing for him, and the degree to which he would follow her example?

Parents who are loyal and loving to each other provide a great sense of strength and security for their children. One elder recalled, "Every day when my dad comes home from work, the first thing he does is give my mom a hug and say, 'I love you.' She says, 'I love you too.' They do it right in front of the door so that everyone can see it. I think they have a very close relationship because of that. We children can see that our parents love each other. When I'm ready to get married, I'll be looking for someone like my mom."

How many times may his mother have felt she didn't measure up in some respect? Did she realize she was providing a model for what her son would look for in an eternal companion?

An elder who had joined the Church in Hong Kong at the age of seventeen appreciated his mother's support and perseverance. "When I was little we had a farm. We always worked together, and she always cared about us and helped us to learn as we were working. It was quite a hard job and she helped us to accomplish our task."

"What kind of work did you do on the farm?" I asked.

"We grew some sort of Chinese flowers. When I was working on the farm I knew I had to finish the job, because if I didn't finish it, my mom would have more work to do. We had a time limit and we had to finish before the sun went down," he said with pride. "That really prepared me to come on a mission. Tracting is not easy sometimes. You just do it and finish the job."

This exemplary elder and his companion once set a goal to knock on 500 doors in a certain length of time. Of that experience, he said, "One night we were thinking, why don't we set a number and then go knock on people's doors? Setting goals is really good; not only is it helping you to achieve something, but after you achieve the goal you have the satisfaction of it. The satisfaction can really help your work and motivate you. So we set a goal. Five hundred. Then we went and knocked. It was really hard."

"Did you reach your goal?"

"Yes, we did. One of the days we were fasting, too. That day we tracted for six hours, and that was hard. But with our focus we did it. It was my mom who taught me not to quit just because you're tired." The lessons shared by a mother in childhood helped prepare a young man to be a stripling warrior who would never quit "just because [he was] tired."

Many of the missionaries spoke of their mothers' love and understanding. One in particular said, "When my friends had problems, they would stop by and talk to my mom for hours. Sometimes I'd come home from work and find one of my friends there talking to my mom. That's because she always understands about what's going on in our lives. Because of that we can trust her. We can talk to her. She shows a lot of love."

Is a mother's work finished when there are no more clothes to wash, meals to fix, and papers to type?

How far does a mother's influence reach? Does the teaching stop when a child leaves the nest? Is a mother's work finished when there are no more clothes to wash, meals to fix, and papers to type? I asked one missionary, "In what ways is your mother's influence affecting you today?"

He explained, "Before I came on my mission there were a couple of things that needed to happen. One thing I needed to do was earn some money, because my family is not well off. I prayed a lot, and I tried to save as much as I could and work as hard as I could. When it came down to being time to go, I didn't have enough. I was concerned.

"Then my mother was able to get a job, and it turned out to be a good one. Because of that, I'm out here. Also my father got a raise on his job—that's a blessing from paying tithing. Sometimes I think about my family back home and I know that my mom is working her heart out so I can be here. I know that God will help and it will work out." This young man did not fear because he had been taught by his mother that if he did not doubt, God would take care of him and his family. His mother's financial contributions were helping to keep him in the mission field, but it was her faithful commitment to training up a child in the way he should go (see Proverbs 22:6) and her example that prepared him to be effective there.

One very sad day we were notified that the mother of one of our missionaries had passed away quite unexpectedly. He had been in the mission field only a few months. He knew he must remain on his mission, and was counseled by the president that it was very possible he would feel near to his mother as he continued in faith and prayer. After several months I asked this young man, "Have there been times when you have felt close to your mom on your mission?"

"Yes, there have," he responded thoughtfully. "Sometimes when I don't do what I'm supposed to, or when I'm doing what I'm supposed to, things that are right, I can feel that someone is there. I don't know how to explain it. Sometimes it feels like somebody is putting their hands on my head or something. It's difficult to explain. I feel that she's around me and she's with me." A mother's influence transcends distance and time and reaches from beyond the veil like a ministering angel.

A mother's love is extended to sons and daughters in the mission field through letters. Missionaries live for the mail, for letters from home. "What kind of letters does your mother write?" I asked one elder.

"Very short and to the point," he answered, "usually because of lack of time. She's the most faithful writer out of the whole family. She's always instructing me and giving me advice: 'Are you being good to your companion; are you representing the Church?' Mothers never change, I guess," he said, his tone of voice implying that he was glad for the consistency.

Another missionary told me his mother wrote "faithfully four times a week. She writes all kinds of letters: spiritual ones, ones when she has felt down. She tells me what everybody's doing and she always tells me what a great missionary and example I've been to the family. I just hope I can live up to that."

"My mom's letters are all uplifting," said another elder. "She just loves missionary work, and she's so excited for any one of her sons to be out on a mission. She usually teaches me something about the gospel. She always bears some type of testimony in her letter."

Those wise mothers recognized a grand opportunity for continuing to teach and love the stripling warriors who were no longer under their protective care in a physical sense. Their support from faraway places lent their sons and daughters an extra measure of strength for the battle on the front lines.

The sacrifice and service of a mother is a quiet labor, often unrecognized until the time of the harvest. But without her gentle, tender, continuous nourishment, the seeds of faith planted in the hearts of her children may lie dormant. Even with her best efforts, fruit may not appear for many seasons.

Good fruit does not all ripen at the same time, and neither do good missionaries. It has been said that anyone who thinks that cherries ripen at the same time as strawberries knows nothing about peaches. So it is with missionaries—each grows in understanding and wisdom at his or her own pace.

One young man seemed to require a little more time than most to grasp the lessons his mother had undoubtedly tried to teach him. He finally was

Seeds of faith, endurance, patience, obedience, and diligence may lie dormant for a time, but once planted they will ultimately take root and one day produce a rich harvest.

awakened and responded after about eighteen months in the mission field. In the season that introduced what became a rich harvest, he wrote, "Dear President: This diligence and obedience stuff is really beginning to kick in." His letters home also revealed his growth, and his mother knew that the lessons had ripened and the fruit was sweet. Young men and women will not remember all the guidance, direction, instruction, and counsel given over the years. Those seeds of faith, endurance, patience, obedience, and diligence may lie dormant for a time, but once planted they will ultimately take root and one day produce a rich harvest.

This process is graphically illustrated by a story told many years ago by Elder LeGrand Richards:

"A country boy was being visited by his city cousin. As the former did his chores, the city boy followed him about. Of course the city boy was curious about some of the things included in these chores. The country boy's life was so different. I don't suppose the city lad knew too much about where milk came from except that they found it on the doorstep each morning. Well, this particular night, the city boy followed the country cousin about while he did his chores. The farm boy took two buckets from the kitchen, one full of milk and the other empty. With the two buckets in hand he moved down toward the corral. Something in the corral smelled the milk in the bucket, started to cut capers in the corral, and by the time the two boys arrived the calf was waiting hysterically for the contents of one of the buckets. The country cousin braced the bucket well with his feet and in a few minutes, the calf had devoured the bucket of milk. The boy took the empty bucket and proceeded to the corner of the corral where the cow was innocently chewing her cud. The country boy sat down and proceeded to milk the cow. The boy from the city was looking on in wonderment at these new experiences: the calf devouring the milk in a hurry and seeing his cousin proceed to pump the cow for the milk. The city boy stepped back, scratched his head and then with delight exclaimed, 'I see, you put it in them when they're young and take it out when they're old'" (Marvin

O. Ashton, *To Whom It May Concern* [Salt Lake City: Bookcraft, 1946], pp. 93–94).

Some children do not readily respond to all the lessons, and some may never conform to the aspirations and dreams of their mothers, but no lesson taught in faith and by example is wasted. It may take months or years, but once a lesson is planted it will stay in a child's heart and come to the fore at a later time.

One mother, Shirley Greene Burnham, wanting to teach in her own way a lesson on listening to the Spirit, composed a poem with this closing stanza:

Listen to your inner drummer;
Step to his quiet beat.
The world beats another rhythm:
A rhythm of defeat.
Let's become a holy people,
Peculiar and divine,
Living in the world,
But walking out of time.

A few short years later, her daughter Rebecca, by this time a mother herself, responded with a poem of her own:

Solid as bedrock 'neath the tempest blast,
Her constant faith taught me to live by hope.
I grew up learning God triumphs at last
Regardless of the Tyrant's powers or scope.
Long and vicious as a struggle may appear,
Exhausting as continued battle be,
Yet I believe, and yet I scorn at fear,
Because I have from her a legacy.
Unwittingly, I've lived by her bright faith,
Remembered not from words, but from her life,
Not knowing that most haven't known such grace,
Have had to face without it all their strife.
An inheritance supreme I gained from Mom—
My great ambition: just to pass it on.

The seeds planted by loving mothers, watered with their tears and nurtured with their patience and faith, produce tender shoots that somehow weather the storms—the harshness of rejection, homesickness, discouragement, and even sometimes despair. In the process a miracle takes place. Is it not a miracle to see a young man or woman newly arrived in the mission field, timid and fearful, with minimal gospel knowledge, soon become bold and courageous in testifying of the Lord Jesus Christ, even in the face of opposition, ridicule, and rejection? To observe young missionaries on their preparation day with their youthful, casual appearance, one would easily forget that they are in the process of becoming spiritual giants. But it is even harder, when they are dressed in their proselyting clothes and one hears them teach and testify, to comprehend that they are only nineteen, twenty, or twenty-one. One is prone to ask, in thoughtful reflection, who are they really? *Whose* are they? Yes, they are children of faithful mothers back home, but also the spiritual offspring of God, their eternal Father, and each one carries a lot of his or her Father inside. Their preparation surely began before they were born, as evidenced by the spirituality expressed in their boldness, their fearlessness, and their faith. Surely one must ask, are these not latter-day stripling warriors?

And what of the leader of these young warriors? As I got more involved in interviewing the young men and women of our mission, it occurred to me one day to inquire of their president, my husband. I sat across the desk from Heber in the mission office and asked him, "What comes to mind when you think of your mother?"

He responded without hesitation, as though he had been anticipating the question. His story was not new to me, of course, but this time I was listening with different intent.

"My mother was left a widow with nine children under fourteen years of age," he began. "She was bedridden most of the time, due to tuberculosis. But I remember we would gather around her bed and she would read stories to us from the Church magazines. And she loved to sing.

"We were in dire poverty, but Mom had a great sense of humor. The sound of her laughter was so contagious when we would tease her." He chuckled aloud at the memory. Then, in a more serious tone, he continued, "Mom insisted that she pay her tithing when she had only pennies to feed a family of nine children. 'We need the Lord's blessings,' she would explain."

As a young man in the military, away from

home, Heber was surrounded by temptation on every side. "How did you handle that?" I asked.

"My mother's trust in me was like bands of steel that could not be broken. I could not think of disappointing my mother," he explained with conviction.

Another time, Heber's desire not to disappoint his mother led him to a life-changing decision. When his older brother was called on a mission, their mother insisted that Heber be called as well, making the source of the necessary finances a matter of faith. "I could not see any possible way I could be supported on a mission," he said, "but my mother had faith that the Lord would provide a way. I could not disappoint my mother."

How different things might have been for this mission president if his mother had not sustained him on his first mission!

After inquiring of so many concerning the things they had learned from their mothers, I found myself drawn in memory to years past, and my mind was flooded with a sense of profound gratitude for my own mother. I realized that she had instilled in me a desire to be good and to treat everyone well. In our little country store, with the Blood Indian reservation on one side of us and a Hutterite colony on the other, we met a variety of people beyond the circle of our family and immediate neighbors. Day after day I watched my mother treat everyone who came into the store with the same dignity, respect, and patience. I can see in my mind's eye the children who would come to make a purchase with only a penny and take ever so long to decide; then when the purchase was made, the candy dropped into a little sack, and the top twisted, they would take yet another look at the many choices and often change their minds. That was quite acceptable to my mother. "People are important," she would say. "They are not just customers; they are our friends." I remember standing at her side behind the counter, watching her tuck into a sack of groceries for a needy family some extra items that she never added to the bill.

Now, years later, when people comment that I am so much like my mother, I think to myself, "Oh, I hope so." In our mission field, where so many different nationalities and cultures were represented, the lessons I learned at my mother's side helped me to see people everywhere as friends.

One mother of a missionary wrote to us, "We gladly and gratefully send our sons on missions. I feel like Hannah. I have lent him to the Lord. As long as he liveth, he shall be lent to the Lord." Another mother, evidently feeling the same way but excited about her son's imminent return, wrote to him, "I pray that you can enjoy your mission up to your very last minute. But I hope you also know you are needed and loved here."

For mothers there are bittersweet tears that flow freely when a child, now grown, waves farewell for a commitment to serve the Lord for eighteen months or two years. Tears are shed and prayers are said and the calendar is marked day by day in anticipation of the missionary's return. Who but a mother can explain the free flow of

Who but a mother can explain the free flow of tears— tears of joy, tears of gratitude, tears of thanksgiving— when her child returns home no longer a boy or a girl, but a man or a woman of God.

tears—tears of joy, tears of gratitude, tears of thanksgiving—when her child returns home no longer a boy or a girl, but a man or a woman of God. We read in the scriptures about how the wise men from the East, directed by a star, went in search of the Christ child. Wicked King Herod instructed the wise men to "go and search diligently for the young child; and when ye have found him, bring me word" (Matthew 2:8). The wise men found the babe, and after paying their homage they followed the promptings of the Spirit and "departed into their own country another way" (Matthew 2:12). Missionaries who teach of Christ, testify of Christ, and follow his example will find him, and in the process find themselves. They will know more of him and come to appreciate more fully his role as their Savior and Redeemer, their advocate with the Father. At the completion of their missions, they, like the wise men, return home another way. A miracle has taken place. The harvest is abundant. The latter-day stripling warriors return to the homes from whence they came, ready to continue on in the work for which they have been prepared.

Considering the honor due the mothers of today's stripling warriors, I am reminded of a speech given by Lucy Mack Smith, the mother of the Prophet Joseph, to a congregation of Saints about to leave Nauvoo for the West after the martyrdom of her sons. Her message was in part as follows: "I raised up eleven children, seven of them boys. I raised them in the fear and love of God. When they were two or three years old I told them I wanted them to love God with all their hearts. I told them to do good. I want all you to do the same. God gives us our children and we are accountable." At the conclusion of her address, she said, "Now, brothers and sisters, if you consider me a Mother in Israel, I want you to say so." Brigham Young invited the audience, "All who consider Mother Smith as a Mother in Israel, signify it by saying yes!" The clerk recorded that "one universal 'Yes' ran through the hall" (Arrington and Madsen, *Mothers of the Prophets,* p. 25).

On July 19, 1995, in the Wilkinson Ballroom

on the Brigham Young University campus, I was speaking to an overflow Education Week audience that included many mothers. Because of inaccurate and incomplete recording on their personal ledgers of success, many of them may have felt inadequate to be considered as mothers in Israel. So I identified today's mothers in Israel, those in the audience "who have in their own way, through faith in God, planted those seeds 'to love God' and 'do good' in their offspring, thus affecting generations." Then I issued an invitation: "All who consider those efforts worthy in qualifying a woman as a mother in Israel, signify by saying 'yes.' Let there be a resounding chorus echoing through generations past, present, and future." A thunderous response echoed through the ballroom, not just once, but twice: "Yes! Yes!" And on that occasion it seemed that the heavens were opened and a chorus of men, women, and children from generations past, present, and future joined in one grand declaration and commendation for our mothers today, "Yes! Yes!" God bless the mothers of today as they prepare the latter-day stripling warriors of tomorrow!